SAY & PRAY
GOD'S WORD

Tracy M. Sumner

SAY & PRAY GOD'S WORD

A Devotional Adventure for Kids

BARBOUR **kidz**

A Division of Barbour Publishing

ISBN 978-1-63609-182-2

Published by Barbour Publishing, Inc., 1810 Barbour Drive, Uhrichsville, Ohio 44683, www.barbourbooks.com

Our mission is to inspire the world with the life-changing message of the Bible.

ECPA Member of the Evangelical Christian Publishers Association

Printed in China.

001523 0323 DS

SAY & PRAY GOD'S WORD!

You know that big book called "the Bible"? Another name for it is "God's Word." We call it that because the Bible is filled with the words God wants us to know.

In His Word, God tells us about Himself and how He made the world. He tells how He made people. . .and how these people went bad by sinning. But God also tells that we can be made right again by believing in His Son, Jesus Christ.

That's one of many promises in the Bible. And that's what this book is all about. When you know the promises in God's Word, you can "say and pray" them back to Him!

This book shows you some of the Bible's most important promises. And it'll encourage you to *memorize* them—to keep them in your heart and mind so that you can say them without even looking.

Then this book will help you *think about* the promises. Short readings called "devotionals" will explain why God's Word is so important to you.

Finally, this book will help you *pray* God's Word. If you take what you've learned and say it back to God in prayer, He will listen. He loves to hear from His kids.

So, are you ready for a big adventure? Keep reading and learning. Then *Say and Pray God's Word*!

1
MEMORIZE!

The Lord is good, a safe place in times of trouble. And He knows those who come to Him to be safe.

NAHUM 1:7

THINK ABOUT!

Have you heard of "good news" and "bad news"?

Bad news means something is wrong. The refrigerator stopped working. Dad's car has a flat tire. You've caught a cold.

Good news is something you *want* to happen. The sun shines when you go to the beach. Mom baked a batch of your favorite cookies. Your best friend stops by to play.

In the Bible, a man named Nahum had good news and bad news. The bad news was that God was angry with a city called Nineveh. People there had been very bad. They were mean and loved hurting everyone around them. They didn't care what God thought. So Nahum told the people God was going to punish them.

But Nahum also shared good news. That news is great to memorize—to say and pray back to God: "The Lord is good, a safe place in times of trouble. And He knows those who come to Him to be safe."

The people of Nineveh ran away from God and got in trouble. But we can choose to run *to* God. When we do, we'll be safe. No matter what's happening—good news or bad—go straight to the Lord. Read His Word, pray to Him, and do what He tells you. He knows who you are, and He will protect you from trouble.

That's good news!

PRAY!

Dear God, Your Word says You are good. You are a safe place in times of trouble. I'm coming to You to be safe, and I know that You know me. Please protect me from scary things. Amen.

2
MEMORIZE!

A gentle answer turns away anger,
but a sharp word causes anger.

Proverbs 15:1

THINK ABOUT!

Can you remember the last time someone said something hurtful to you? Maybe it was an angry brother, sister, classmate, or friend. It didn't feel good, did it? It probably made you so mad that you wanted to say something mean in return.

The Bible has some advice for those times you feel like answering unkind words with unkind words of your own: don't do it! One Bible writer said it this way: "When someone does something bad to you, do not do the same thing to him" (1 Peter 3:9).

God's Word has a lot to say about the words we use. It teaches us to always tell the truth, even when it's hard. But the Bible also says we should speak to others with gentleness and kindness, even when they've been nasty to us.

Your kind, gentle words can help and encourage others. They can help you build good friendships. Even better, your words can bring others closer to Jesus.

But unkind words? They just cause anger and ruin your friendships.

So when you're about to speak to the people God has placed in your life, first stop and think. Then say and pray, "A gentle answer turns away anger, but a sharp word causes anger."

PRAY!

Dear Lord, I sometimes say mean things to others—even to people I love. Help me to think before I hurt anyone with my words. Help me to only say things that are kind and helpful to others. Amen.

3
MEMORIZE!

The man who gives much will have much, and he who helps others will be helped himself.

PROVERBS 11:25

THINK ABOUT!

God wants you to give to others. He wants you to give happily and *generously*—which just means you never worry about whether you're giving away too much. Second Corinthians 9:7 says, "Each man should give as he has decided in his heart. He should not give, wishing he could keep it. Or he should not give if he feels he has to give. God loves a man who gives because he wants to give."

As a young kid, you may not be able to give a lot of money. But this is still a good time to learn how important it is to give. It's also good to learn that God promises to do great things for you when you give from what you have.

Yes, God wants you to give. But He wants you to give because you want to. . .not because you think you have to. When you give like that, God will notice. And He promises to *bless* you—to do good things for you.

If you see a person who needs something that you can give, think about Proverbs 11:25. Then say and pray, "The man who gives much will have much, and he who helps others will be helped himself."

How can you give happily and generously today?

PRAY!

Dear God, You want me to learn how to give. Thank You for promising to bless me when I give to others in need. Amen.

4
MEMORIZE!

Be wise in the way you live around those who are not Christians. Make good use of your time. Speak with them in such a way they will want to listen to you.

Colossians 4:5–6

THINK ABOUT!

Do you think you set a good example of how a Christian should live and talk? Do you stay away from sin and treat people the way Jesus wants you to? Are there some places in your heart that could use some extra work?

As a Christian, you shouldn't be the same as people who don't yet know Jesus. You should think, act, and treat people differently. That's because Jesus' Holy Spirit lives inside you. He's changing you into a different person than you were before.

Today's Bible verses say that others should always be able to see God working in us. These verses tell us that we should be careful to live the way God wants us to. That way, we'll be great examples of those who follow Jesus. We should speak in ways that make people want to listen.

Jesus wants you to tell others what He's done for you. If you want to make God happy by the way you live and talk, say and pray these words: "Be wise in the way you live around those who are not Christians. Make good use of your time. Speak with them in such a way they will want to listen to you."

PRAY!

Jesus, I want to tell others about You. I know that means I need to live and talk in ways that make You happy. Please help me to be the kind of person that people will listen to when I talk about You. Amen.

5
MEMORIZE!

If you respect your father and mother, you will live a long time and your life will be full of many good things.

Ephesians 6:3

THINK ABOUT!

The Bible teaches that you should do what your mom and dad ask you to do. (Look up Proverbs 1:8 and Ephesians 6:1!) But the Bible doesn't stop there—it also says to *respect* them.

Respecting your parents means more than just doing what they ask you to do. It's possible for you to obey them 100 percent yet not show them any respect.

Let's say Mom tells you to turn off the TV and go clean your room. You might clean your room top to bottom and in every direction. But if you drag your feet, make ugly faces, and grumble on your way to your bedroom, you haven't respected your mom.

God doesn't like that! That's why you should say and pray, "If you respect your father and mother, you will live a long time and your life will be full of many good things."

Respecting your parents means treating them like they're important. It means realizing that God made you as their son or daughter. And it means going beyond just obeying them when they ask you to do something. It means doing it happily, as if you're doing it for the Lord.

You may not enjoy cleaning your room. Or taking out the trash. Or doing the dishes after dinner. But when Mom or Dad ask you to do those things, you make God happy when you do them with a smile.

PRAY!

Dear Lord, thank You for my mom and dad. In the Bible, You promise that good things happen to kids who respect their parents. Help me to always respect my parents in the things I say and do. Amen.

6
MEMORIZE!

Keep awake! Watch at all times.
The devil is working against you.
He is walking around like a hungry
lion with his mouth open. He is
looking for someone to eat.

1 PETER 5:8

THINK ABOUT!

The Bible says that the devil is always sneaking around looking for someone to tempt. But you don't have to be afraid of him. The Bible says, "Stand against the devil and he will run away from you" (James 4:7). If you resist the devil, he can't stay!

How can you resist him? By reading your Bible and asking God to give you the strength to say no when the devil tries to tempt you to sin. The Bible teaches that the more you know what the Word says, the easier it'll be to resist temptation. That's why the Bible says, "Your Word have I hid in my heart, that I may not sin against You" (Psalm 119:11).

God's Word is a powerful weapon that can fight against the devil's lies. Jesus set a great example of how we can use the Bible's words to win against temptation. You can read all about how Jesus sent the devil running in Matthew 4:1–11. All it took was a few words from the Bible!

The devil is a sneaky, powerful enemy who will stop at nothing to convince you to sin. But you can beat Him. Start by saying and praying, "Keep awake! Watch at all times. The devil is working against you. He is walking around like a hungry lion with his mouth open. He is looking for someone to eat."

PRAY!

Dear Lord, Your Words in the Bible teach me how to live in a way that makes You happy. Help me to understand the Bible better and better each day so that I can stand against the devil when he tries to tempt me to do wrong.

7

MEMORIZE!

A little with the fear of the Lord is better than great riches with trouble.

PROVERBS 15:16

THINK ABOUT!

Have you ever wished your family had lots of money? Most kids probably do! You might want a better bicycle. A family vacation to a place far away would be great, wouldn't it? And who wouldn't love to go out to dinner every night?

There's nothing wrong with having money. But the Bible says that being *content* with having God— even if you don't have anything else—is better than having a lot of money but not having Him.

The word *content* means feeling happy with what you have. It means thinking, "I wouldn't mind having more, but I'm happy with what I have." That's what the Bible means when it says, "A God-like life gives us much when we are happy for what we have" (1 Timothy 6:6).

God may choose to bless your family with more money. But He may not. Either way, thank Him every day for what He's given you and your family. Say and pray, "A little with the fear of the Lord is better than great riches with trouble."

PRAY!

Dear God, You promised to take care of me and my family. So whenever I start thinking of how much better life would be if we had nicer things, remind me to be content with what You have given me. Amen.

8

MEMORIZE!

"I will show loving-kindness to them and forgive their sins. I will remember their sins no more."

HEBREWS 8:12

THINK ABOUT!

It might seem funny to think that God forgets things. God knows everything. He always has and always will. So how can He forget something?

Hebrews 8:12 says that when God forgives you for something you've done wrong, He also chooses to forget about it. That means that to Him, it's as if these mistakes never happened.

Isn't that great?

It's really hard to forget the past after you've done something wrong, and it's even harder when someone else has hurt you. But not for God. When you mess up, God still loves you and wants to forgive you.

Jesus came to earth to live a perfect life and to teach people how to make God happy. Then, when the time was right, Jesus gave up His life—taking your punishment—so that God could forgive you for the wrong things you've done. And once God has forgiven you, your sins are gone forever!

You might still remember a time when you disobeyed God. Maybe you still feel bad when you think about it. If so, say and pray God's own words: "I will show loving-kindness to them and forgive their sins. I will remember their sins no more."

PRAY!

*Dear God, thank You for choosing
to forget all the wrong things I
have done. I may still remember
those things, but You don't.
You've promised to forgive my sins
whenever I tell You I'm sorry.*

9
MEMORIZE!

"For sure, I tell you, he who puts his trust in Me has life that lasts forever."

John 6:47

THINK ABOUT!

What does the word *forever* mean to you? Another word for forever is *eternity*, which means "without end." Forever is a long, long time—longer than you can possibly imagine.

It's hard for us to understand eternity—at least while we're living here on earth. That's because every living thing on this earth has a start and an end. Every bird, animal, fish, plant, and human had a start and will die one day. Even the earth itself will come to an end!

But did you know that God created you to be a *forever* person? Even though your body will stop working someday, that part that makes you *you* will go on forever and ever. And because you trust in Jesus and follow Him, you'll spend forever with Him in a wonderful place called heaven.

Just think about it! The Bible includes thousands of great promises from God to people who love and follow Him. That includes this wonderful promise that you can say and pray: "For sure, I tell you, he who puts his trust in Me has life that lasts forever."

Doesn't that make you want to do everything you can to make sure your friends and family members are there with you?

PRAY!

God, You promised that when I put my trust in Jesus, I'll have a never-ending life in heaven with You. That's the best thing anyone has ever said to me! Thank You for that amazing promise. Amen.

10
MEMORIZE!

*Your Word is a lamp to my feet
and a light to my path.*

PSALM 119:105

THINK ABOUT!

If you've ever walked through the woods without a flashlight during a dark night, then you know how scary it can be. When you can't see two feet in front of you, you can easily trip over rocks and sticks and end up face-down in the dirt with skinned-up knees and elbows. Ouch!

The Bible teaches that the world you live in now is a lot like that scary, dark path. Sin makes this world dark. That means you'll need some kind of light in order to see the path in front of you. When you have that light, you won't trip and fall.

The writer of Psalm 119 says that this light is the Bible. He says, "Your Word is a lamp to my feet and a light to my path." In other words, the Bible gives you what you need so that you can go through life without tripping into sin. And it's something you can say and pray every day!

This world can be a scary place. But when you trust the promises in God's Word, you have nothing to fear as you walk the path He has for you.

PRAY!

Dear God, I know I can depend on You to keep Your promises I read about in the Bible. Thank You for always doing what You promise to do—including giving me the light I need each day. Amen.

11
MEMORIZE!

"I am the Lord your God Who holds your right hand, and Who says to you, 'Do not be afraid. I will help you.' "

Isaiah 41:13

THINK ABOUT!

Can you remember a time when you were in a scary place. . .but you weren't afraid because your dad or mom was right there with you, holding your hand? You just knew everything was going to be okay, didn't you?

Speaking through a man named Isaiah, God promised to do the same thing for His people. He told the people of Israel, "Do not be afraid. I will help you." God wanted the people to know He was big and strong enough to help and protect them. But He also wanted them to know He loved them enough to do it.

Everyone feels afraid sometimes. You probably have too! Maybe you wanted to try out for a team, but you were too afraid of not making it. Fear can keep you from doing great things—including the things you know God wants you to do.

When you feel afraid or worried over something, just imagine yourself holding God's hand. Say and pray to God, "I am the Lord your God Who holds your right hand, and Who says to you, 'Do not be afraid. I will help you.' "

PRAY!

*Lord, this world can be a dark place,
especially for kids. But Your Word
shows me that I don't have to let
anything scare me. That's because
You always hold my hand and help
me through the bad times. Amen.*

12
MEMORIZE!

*We are [God's] work. He has
made us to belong to Christ
Jesus so we can work for Him.
He planned that we should do this.*

EPHESIANS 2:10

THINK ABOUT!

Do you want to do good things for God? Do you want to love others in many wonderful ways? Do you want to show them how much God loves them and how He can change their lives?

If you want to do all those things, great! God wants you to do them too!

God created you and saved you so that you could do good things for Him and for others. He gave you this mission before you were even born.

God has given you gifts and talents so that you can use them to serve Him. He wants you to use those gifts and talents to help people and to introduce them to Jesus. When you do that, you show others how amazing Jesus is!

So how do you find out what God wants you to do? The best way to start is by staying as close to Him as possible. You do that by reading your Bible every day and by talking to Him whenever you have the chance. You can even say and pray, "We are [God's] work. He has made us to belong to Christ Jesus so we can work for Him. He planned that we should do this."

When you do those things, He will show you the good things He wants You to do. Not only that, He'll give you the power to do things you could never do on your own!

PRAY!

Dear God, thank You for preparing good things for me to do—long before I was even born. I want to do what You want me to. Please use me to help others know how wonderful You are. Amen.

13
MEMORIZE!

"If you forgive people their sins, your Father in heaven will forgive your sins also."

MATTHEW 6:14

THINK ABOUT!

You probably already know this, but people will sometimes do and say things that make you feel hurt and upset. Sometimes, you feel angry at other people for their mean words and actions.

When those things happen—when you feel angry at a friend, your brother or sister, or even your mom or dad—what do you think God wants you to do?

The Bible says a lot about forgiveness. It says that Jesus died for our mistakes so that God could forgive us. It says that when we confess the wrong we have done, God washes us clean of our dirty sin. But it also says that God wants us to forgive others when they hurt us or make us angry.

Forgiving others is *very* important to God. To help yourself remember this, you can say and pray Jesus' words: "If you forgive people their sins, your Father in heaven will forgive your sins also."

God wants to make you more and more like Jesus every day. As He helps you to grow into the person He wants you to be, you'll find it easier to forgive people, even when they don't deserve it.

When you forgive others, you're doing what Jesus did for you!

PRAY!

Dear God, people aren't very nice to me sometimes. But instead of getting mad—or trying to get even— I want to forgive those who have hurt me. . .just like You forgive me when I make You unhappy. Amen.

14
MEMORIZE!

I am sure that God Who began the good work in you will keep on working in you until the day Jesus Christ comes again.

PHILIPPIANS 1:6

THINK ABOUT!

Have you ever started without finishing? Maybe you started a beautiful jigsaw puzzle, but you gave up when you found it was too hard. Or maybe you quit after your room was halfway clean because something else distracted you. (Mom wasn't too happy, was she?)

It's not always easy to finish what we start. It's even harder when we don't really care about what we're doing.

You'll be happy to know that God isn't like that! He always finishes what He starts, even when it takes *lots* of time and work.

Philippians 1:6 says that He won't give up on you, no matter what. It says that He will finish what He started when He first saved you from sin. So say and pray, "I am sure that God Who began the good work in you will keep on working in you until the day Jesus Christ comes again."

We humans sometimes quit on something halfway because it's too hard. But nothing is too hard for God. He'll never give up on you, and He is able to make you into the person He wants you to be. Even better, He never gets distracted! He keeps His full attention on you because He loves you more than you can understand.

PRAY!

Dear God, I sometimes hear my mom or dad talking about how my body is growing so fast. I hope they can also see that I'm growing as a kid who has chosen to follow You. Thank You for working to make me the kind of Christian You want me to be. Amen.

15
MEMORIZE!

The Lord is my rock, and my safe place, and the One Who takes me out of trouble. My God is my rock, in Whom I am safe. He is my safe-covering, my saving strength, and my strong tower.

PSALM 18:2

THINK ABOUT!

David, the man God had chosen to be the second king of Israel, wrote Psalm 18 after God had saved him from His enemies, including King Saul. David had known all along that God was big and powerful enough to keep him safe, but in this psalm, he praised God for doing what he always knew the Lord could do.

God loves you, and He always wants to be your source of safety. Nothing surprises God. He knows when you're tempted. He knows when you feel sad or worried. He knows when you're mad or scared. He knows everything about you, and He promises to be with you through it all.

That's why the Bible says, "Be strong with the Lord's strength" (Ephesians 6:10). And it's why you can say and pray, "The Lord is my rock, and my safe place, and the One Who takes me out of trouble. My God is my rock, in Whom I am safe."

When you feel tempted to do wrong, go to your Father in heaven. And when you feel sad or discouraged, run to God. The safest place you could ever be is in His loving arms. He promises to never let go of you or to allow anything to harm you.

And when God helps you out, don't forget to praise and thank Him for being your source of safety.

PRAY!

Dear Lord, whenever I am tempted, sad, or afraid, You're the only one I can trust to keep me safe. . .so remind me to run to You. Thank You for being so strong. Amen.

16
MEMORIZE!

*For if a man belongs to Christ,
he is a new person. The old life
is gone. New life has begun.*

2 CORINTHIANS 5:17

THINK ABOUT!

"Metamorphosis." Wow, *that's* a long word! But don't worry—this fancy word just means a change from one thing to another. In nature, metamorphosis happens when a squirmy, ugly caterpillar changes into a beautiful, colorful butterfly.

As awesome as that is, God does something far better for everyone who becomes a Christian. God takes people who are filled with ugly, dirty sin, and He makes them brand new—He even gives them a new life! These people may look the same and have the same personality, but the way they think and live is changed forever. Jesus lives in them now, and He changes everything from the inside out.

A caterpillar changing into a butterfly is wonderful. But the way God brings new life to a person who's dead on the inside because of sin? That's a miracle! And that's not all. After a person becomes a Christian, God continues working inside that person. Over time, the Christian thinks more like God thinks and lives more like God wants His children to live. Out with the old life, in with the new!

So say it and pray it: "For if a man belongs to Christ, he is a new person. The old life is gone. New life has begun."

PRAY!

Jesus, thank You for making me new on the inside. Thank You for throwing out the ugly, sinful part of me and putting in Your goodness. You've done what I could never, ever do for myself—You've made me clean and sin-free in Your eyes. Amen.

17
MEMORIZE!

*"If anyone wants to be first,
he must be last of all. He will
be the one to care for all."*

MARK 9:35

THINK ABOUT!

One day, Jesus and His twelve closest followers were traveling to a town called Capernaum. As they walked, the disciples began arguing about which of them was the most important. Jesus knew what they were arguing about, but He still asked them, "What were you arguing about along the road?"

His followers, feeling embarrassed, just looked at the ground. Then Jesus told them something that you too can say and pray: "If anyone wants to be first, he must be last of all. He will be the one to care for all."

There's nothing wrong with wanting to be the best player on the soccer team. And there's also nothing wrong with wanting to have the best score on a test. But Jesus said it's much more important to be *humble*—which just means you are nice and helpful to everyone and put others before yourself.

Being last doesn't mean you aren't important to God. It just means that you treat everyone like they are more important than you are. It means doing things that make others feel happy. It means encouraging sad people and sharing what you have with those who are in need.

Do you want to be important in God's kingdom? Then start by putting others first!

PRAY!

Lord Jesus, help me to always put others ahead of myself and to care for people every day. I know that's the kind of kid You want me to be. Amen.

18
MEMORIZE!

You will show me the way of life. Being with You is to be full of joy. In Your right hand there is happiness forever.

Psalm 16:11

THINK ABOUT!

What do you think the word *joy* means? Maybe you think it means the same thing as "happiness." That's a good guess, but these two are not quite the same. Happiness is what you feel when something good happens to you. You feel happy when you get a new bicycle for your birthday or when Mom or Dad promise to take the whole family on a great vacation. But joy is different. You don't have to feel happy to feel joy.

David, the writer of Psalm 16, didn't have a perfect life. He made many mistakes and many bad things happened to him. Everywhere he went, people wanted to hurt him. Sometimes, he felt sad and even scared. But David never stopped trusting God or living the way God wanted Him to. That's why he could say and pray, "Being with You is to be full of joy."

So can you!

Each day, you can have joy inside you, even when you feel sad or unhappy. One day, you'll be in heaven, where you'll feel happy *all* the time! For now, you can always feel joy by just thinking about how much God loves you and wants to be with you. . .and how much He has done for you.

PRAY!

Father in heaven, thank You for being so good to me. Thank You for blessing me in so many ways and for leading me into Your way of life. Being with You brings me joy, even in the hard times. Amen.

19
MEMORIZE!

The fear of the Lord makes life longer.

THINK ABOUT!

Have you ever heard of a person who "fears the Lord"? The Bible talks about many people who feared God—and it always means something good. Not only that, the Bible tells us that fearing God will help us in many ways.

But what does "fearing God" mean? Does it mean you should be afraid of God like you'd be afraid of a big, mean dog? Does it mean God is some kind of scary monster who's just waiting for you to mess up so that He can jump on you?

No, God isn't like that at all! God is bigger and more powerful than you can imagine, and He made the world you see around you. But even better, God has also told us in the Bible that He is a kind heavenly Father who loves you beyond your best dreams.

Does that sound like someone to be afraid of? Of course not! Instead, you should have a deep respect for God, understanding that He sees and knows everything about you—even what you're thinking right now. That's why you can say and pray, "The fear of the Lord makes life longer."

God is good and kind, and He wants you to love Him and feel free to talk to Him—not to feel scared of Him.

PRAY!

Dear God, help me to always give You the love and respect You deserve. When I do that, I'll live in a way that makes You happy. That's the best way to live! Amen.

20
MEMORIZE!

The heavens are telling of the greatness of God and the great open spaces above show the work of His hands.

PSALM 19:1

THINK ABOUT!

If you want to get an idea of how big and powerful God really is, all you have to do is step outside and look into the night sky. See all the stars and the moon? God made those! In fact, He made much, much more. In our part of the universe, called the Milky Way galaxy, He made hundreds of billions of stars. We can hardly imagine such big numbers. And He made even more galaxies!

Thinking about these things can make you feel really, really small. It can cause you to say and pray, "The heavens are telling of the greatness of God and the great open spaces above show the work of His hands."

Thousands of years ago, a man named David looked up and saw the moon and stars. Just then, he was overwhelmed by a single thought—the same God who made all of this also thought about him and loved him so much:

When I look up and think about Your heavens, the work of Your fingers, the moon and the stars, which You have set in their place, what is man, that You think of him, the son of man that You care for him? (Psalm 8:3–4)

That's a cool thought, isn't it? It makes you want to just open your mouth and praise God for His greatness. . .and for His goodness to you.

PRAY!

Dear Lord, all I have to do to get an idea of how awesome You are is look up and see the stars and galaxies You've put out in space. And all I have to do to get an idea of how good You are is think about how much You love me. Amen.

21
MEMORIZE!

"For God so loved the world that He gave His only Son. Whoever puts his trust in God's Son will not be lost but will have life that lasts forever."

JOHN 3:16

THINK ABOUT!

John 3:16 is the best-known verse in the Bible. It's the *gospel* or "good news" in an easy-to-understand form.

Here is everything John 3:16 says:

- *For God so loved*: The Bible says that "God is love" (1 John 4:16). Everything He does comes from His love.

- *The world*: The "world" is all the people who live on this planet. That includes you, your family, and everyone else you know.

- *That He gave*: God loves, so He gives. That's what love does!

- *His only Son*: God sent His Son, Jesus, to live here on earth and then die for your sins so that you could be forgiven.

- *Whoever puts his trust in God's Son*: A person is saved by trusting Jesus, God's Son!

- *Will not be lost but will have life that lasts forever*: Jesus wants you to live with Him in a forever home called heaven.

Whenever you pray, don't forget to thank God for giving you Jesus. Say and pray, "God so loved the world that He gave His only Son. Whoever puts his trust in God's Son will not be lost but will have life that lasts forever." Also, ask Him to help you tell others about Him so that they can go to heaven too.

PRAY!

Lord, thank You for loving me enough to send Jesus to die for my sin so that I could be forgiven and live in heaven forever. Please help me to tell others about what You've done for them too. Amen.

22
MEMORIZE!

"You must love the Lord your God with all your heart and with all your soul and with all your strength."

DEUTERONOMY 6:5

THINK ABOUT!

One day, someone asked Jesus which one of the Old Testament laws was most important. Jesus quoted Deuteronomy 6:5: "'You must love the Lord your God with all your heart and with all your soul and with all your mind.' This is the first and greatest of the Laws" (Matthew 22:37–38).

This commandment is the most important because when you love God with everything you have, then you'll *want* to do the things that make Him happy. . .and avoid all the things that don't. If you love God, you'll worship only Him. If you love God, you won't use His name wrongly. If you love God, you'll respect and obey your mom and dad. If you love God, you'll love others and treat them the way God wants you to.

Jesus once said to His followers, "If you love Me, you will do what I say" (John 14:15). He loved you so much that He chose to die on the cross so that you could be forgiven for the wrong things you've done—and so that you can live in heaven with Him forever. When you love Jesus in return, you'll happily do everything He wants you to do.

So today, say and pray, "You must love the Lord your God with all your heart and with all your soul and with all your strength."

PRAY!

Dear Lord, the Bible teaches that You loved me before I was even born. It says You even loved me enough to send Jesus to earth so that I could live forever in heaven. Help me to love You in return with my whole heart. Amen.

23
MEMORIZE!

*"Do what is right and good
in the eyes of the Lord.
Then it will be well with you."*

DEUTERONOMY 6:18

THINK ABOUT!

Before the Israelites, God's chosen people, moved into the land God had given them, Moses reminded them of how they could make God happy. In Deuteronomy 6:18, he said, "Do what is right and good in the eyes of the Lord. Then it will be well with you."

Doing what is right and good in the eyes of the Lord isn't as hard as you might think. You can make God happy if you do these three simple things:

- *Read your Bible every day.* That way, you'll know what God wants from you and how He wants you to live. The Bible is an important book that tells you everything you need to know about making God happy with you.

- *Pray all the time.* God loves it when you take time to talk to Him. When you pray, tell God how thankful you are for everything He's done for you. Tell Him what you need. Pray for other people and ask God to bless them too.

- *Love God with all your heart and love other people.* Jesus taught that these were the two greatest Old Testament laws (Matthew 22:36–40). That's because when you love God and other people the way God wants you too, all the other laws will fall into place.

Yes! It really is that simple! And so is saying and praying, "Do what is right and good in the eyes of the Lord. Then it will be well with you."

PRAY!

*Dear Lord, thank You for leading me
and telling me what You want me to do.
I love You, so I want to make You happy
with me. I also want all the good things
You have promised to give me. Amen.*

24
MEMORIZE!

Do not let yourselves get tired of doing good. If we do not give up, we will get what is coming to us at the right time.

GALATIANS 6:9

THINK ABOUT!

Sometimes, it's easy to feel discouraged as you try to do what God wants you to. You know He wants you to be kind and loving to everyone—including those who don't follow Jesus. You know He wants you to pray that these people will be saved. And you've been telling someone about Jesus for a while now, but that person's life hasn't changed.

Sometimes you obey God but it doesn't seem to make any difference. You might feel sad and hopeless. Maybe you just want to give up!

If you feel that way, read and memorize—and say and pray—Galatians 6:9: "Do not let yourselves get tired of doing good. If we do not give up, we will get what is coming to us at the right time."

God calls us to one thing before anything else: faithfulness. Being faithful to God means not giving up, even when no one else seems to notice. It means continuing to love others and show kindness every chance you get. It means telling others about Jesus and praying for them every day.

So don't get tired. . .and don't give up! When the time is right, God will reward you for your faithfulness.

PRAY!

God, You promise to give great things to those who do good in Your name. Give me strength so that I can do good for You— and for others—every day. Amen.

25
MEMORIZE!

But the fruit that comes from having the Holy Spirit in our lives is: love, joy, peace, not giving up, being kind, being good, having faith, being gentle, and being the boss over our own desires.

GALATIANS 5:22–23

THINK ABOUT!

The verses you just read offer a long list of the fruits of the Spirit. But what exactly are these "fruits"? Well, they're the good things God does in us when we trust in Him and allow His Holy Spirit to work inside us so that people can tell that we love Jesus.

Here's how it works.

Think of yourself as a tree. But this is no ordinary tree—it's a tree that grows all kinds of delicious fruit. One branch grows tasty, crispy apples. Another branch grows sweet, juicy oranges. There's a pear branch, a banana branch, a peach branch. . .and a branch for every other fruit you can think of.

In order for a tree like you to grow fruit, it would need sunlight, water, and good dirt. Without those things, the fruit wouldn't grow. But with them, you'd produce lots and lots of yummy stuff!

That's what the Holy Spirit does for you. When you trust God and allow His Spirit to work in you, you'll bear all kinds of wonderful fruit for Him. He will shine His light on you, water you, and plant you in good soil so that you can grow the fruit He wants you to grow. So say and pray, "But the fruit that comes from having the Holy Spirit in our lives is: love, joy, peace, not giving up, being kind, being good, having faith, being gentle, and being the boss over our own desires."

PRAY!

Lord, You've given me Your Holy Spirit so that my life will make You happy. I want to be a loving, patient, kind, gentle kid who has strong faith in You. I know the Holy Spirit will make me that kind of person. Amen.

26
MEMORIZE!

I will give thanks to You, for the greatness of the way I was made brings fear. Your works are great and my soul knows it very well.

PSALM 139:14

THINK ABOUT!

When you look in the mirror, what do you see? At first, you might not notice anything special. You're just an ordinary kid, right?

But take a closer look. Go ahead! What color is your hair? Your eyes? How tall are you? Now think about the things that make you *you*. Are you funny, smart, or athletic? What do you like to do for fun? Do you like being in big groups of people, or is hanging out with just a couple of close friends good enough for you?

There's a lot more to you than you first thought, isn't there? You really are one of a kind. That's because God created you to be just who you are. He's made billions of people, but He only made one *you*! He chose your hair and eye color, your skin tone, your height, and everything about you.

God made you truly one-of-a-kind. And even if there are some things about yourself that you'd like to change, you don't need to be anything other than what God made you to be. God made you, so you can say and pray, "I will give thanks to You, for the greatness of the way I was made brings fear. Your works are great and my soul knows it very well."

PRAY!

Dear Lord, thank You for making me who I am. When You put me together, You paid close attention to every detail. You made me to love You, to know You personally, and to be the kid You want me to be. Amen.

27
MEMORIZE!

*If we tell Him our sins, He is faithful
and we can depend on Him to
forgive us of our sins. He will make
our lives clean from all sin.*

1 JOHN 1:9

THINK ABOUT!

What if a good friend came over to your house to play, but that friend had just spent time crawling around in a stinky pig pen? You'd still be glad to see your friend, but you wouldn't want to get too close—at least not until your friend took a bath. . .with lots and lots of soap!

It's kind of like that with God, but with one big difference: He doesn't care about how dirty and stinky our bodies are. God cares about what's *inside* us. And the more we do things that make Him unhappy with us, the further away from Him we'll start to feel.

When you do something wrong, you don't stop being God's child. He loves you, and He won't let you go. Instead, God offers to forgive you and wash out all your sin. All you need to do is tell Him that you've done wrong and ask Him to forgive you.

We all do things that make God unhappy. But the moment you tell Him you're sorry, He promises to forgive you and cleanse you. So don't wait around! Just say and pray, "If we tell Him our sins, He is faithful and we can depend on Him to forgive us of our sins. He will make our lives clean from all sin."

PRAY!

Dear God, thank You for forgiving me when I do something wrong. I know I'll never be perfect. . .at least not until I'm in heaven with You. But I also know that when I admit my sin to You, You'll forgive me and clean me up so that I can be close to You. Amen.

28
MEMORIZE!

*The next day John the Baptist
saw Jesus coming to him. He said,
"See! The Lamb of God Who takes
away the sin of the world!"*

John 1:29

THINK ABOUT!

What do you think of when you see a cute baby lamb? You probably think it looks pure, innocent, and unable to hurt anyone, right? But does it remind you of Jesus? It should!

In Old Testament times, God told people to *sacrifice* (kill) a perfect, innocent lamb so that they could have their sins forgiven. The lamb took their punishment.

But God had planned from the beginning to send Jesus to earth so that He could be the perfect, once-and-for-all sacrifice for our sins. That's why when a man called John the Baptist saw Jesus, he called Him "the Lamb of God."

Right now, you might be thinking, *It's not fair! Why should a perfect, pure man have to die? Wasn't there another way?* The answer, sadly, is no. It was the only way God could make us clean.

Jesus never sinned. He lived a perfect life here on earth. That's why He was the only one whose sacrifice could wash away our sins. And thanks to Him, we can live forever with God in heaven!

So thank Him every day. . .and say and pray, "See! The Lamb of God Who takes away the sin of the world!"

PRAY!

Dear Jesus, thank You for being the perfect, sinless Lamb of God. God sent You to earth to die on a wooden cross so that my sins could be taken away— You were the only one who could do it. Thank You for giving Your life for me.

29
MEMORIZE!

This is the day that the Lord has made.
Let us be full of joy and be glad in it.

PSALM 118:24

THINK ABOUT!

What is the first thing you do when your alarm clock goes off in the morning—or when your mom ruffles your hair and tells you it's time to get up?

Some of us like to pop out of bed every morning with an "up and at 'em" attitude. Others are. . .less excited. (Just a few more minutes, Mom!) No matter what kind of kid you are in the morning, the writer of Psalm 118:24 gives you words you can say and pray every day when you open your eyes: "This is the day that the Lord has made. Let us be full of joy and be glad in it."

Each new day is a wonderful gift from God that brings you new beginnings and new chances to do nice things for other people, to make new friends, to listen to God, and to do the things He wants you to do.

When you wake up in the morning, you get to open your mouth and thank God for another day and ask Him how You can make Him happy. Start your day by choosing to be joyful from the moment you get out of bed. That's the best way to begin!

PRAY!

Dear God, help me to see each new day as a gift from You. When I wake up every morning, remind me to thank You for another day and for what You have done for me. Amen.

30
MEMORIZE!

"You are the light of the world. You cannot hide a city that is on a mountain."

MATTHEW 5:14

THINK ABOUT!

Have you ever sung the old song "This Little Light of Mine" in Sunday school or children's church? It goes like this:

This little light of mine, I'm gonna let it shine

Let it shine, let it shine, let it shine.

Everywhere I go, I'm gonna let it shine

Let it shine, let it shine, let it shine.

Because you follow Jesus, you have the light from this song inside you. He wants you to let that light shine in this dark world, letting everyone know how wonderful it is to follow Jesus.

Jesus was the light of the world when He was on earth, but He told His followers that once He returned to heaven, it'd be their turn to shine. That means we get to obey Jesus in front of others and also tell them about Him. And it means you can say and pray, "You are the light of the world. You cannot hide a city that is on a mountain."

How can you shine your light in this dark world? You can start by praying for other Christians and for people who don't yet trust in Jesus. You can also do nice things for others, not because you want anything in return but because you want to help people and *glorify* (give all the attention to) God. And you can also tell others about Jesus!

You have the light of Jesus inside you. Make sure you let it shine so that others can see it!

PRAY!

Lord Jesus, I want my family and friends to see me as an example of what truly following You looks like. But I know I can't do that on my own. Please give me everything I need to live the way You want me to live and to love people the way You love them. Help me shine for You! Amen.

31
MEMORIZE!

Dear friends, let us love each other, because love comes from God. Those who love are God's children and they know God.

1 JOHN 4:7

THINK ABOUT!

The apostle John, who wrote today's verse, knew about God's love for him. After all, he spent three years with Jesus when He was on earth, and he often called himself "the disciple Jesus loved" in the Gospel of John.

God showed His heart of love for us when He sent His Son, Jesus, to live as a man on earth and then die on the cross so that we could be forgiven for our sin. And that love flows from God's heart toward us every day.

But God doesn't just shower us with His love so that we can keep it to ourselves. He wants us to share that love with others. He wants us to love others because He loved us first. And He wants us to love not just through what we say but through what we do. That's what the Bible means when it says, "My children, let us not love with words or in talk only. Let us love by what we do and in truth" (1 John 3:18).

There are all kinds of ways you can show God's love to your mom or dad, your other relatives, and your friends. So today, think of some ways to do that—then do them! Say and pray, "Let us love each other, because love comes from God. Those who love are God's children and they know God."

PRAY!

Dear Lord, I know You want me to love others. Loving people shows that I know You as my Father in heaven. Help me find ways to love others just as You love me. Amen.

32
MEMORIZE!

"First of all, look for the holy nation of God. Be right with Him. All these other things will be given to you also."

MATTHEW 6:33

THINK ABOUT!

There are probably a lot of things in your life that are very important to you. And as you grow and become a teenager and then an adult, the things you find important will start to change. (Trust us on that one!)

That's why it's important that you learn now that the most important thing in your life should be God and His kingdom. And that's why Jesus told His followers something you can say and pray: "First of all, look for the holy nation of God. Be right with Him. All these other things will be given to you also."

Having important things in your life is not wrong. Neither is loving your mom and dad, sisters or brothers, other family members, and close friends. God put these people in your life, and He wants you to love them. It's also not wrong to value your time being part of a team and going out to play with your friends.

But God wants you to put all those important things far behind your relationship with Him. Don't let anything, even the important things, take your eyes off Jesus, who loves you so much that He gave His life for you.

PRAY!

Dear Lord, You've promised all of Your children that You will give us what we need in this life. Help me not to worry about what I need—instead, help me focus on being right with You and serving You every day. Amen.

33
MEMORIZE!

Let us put every thing out of our lives that keeps us from doing what we should. Let us keep running in the race that God has planned for us.

HEBREWS 12:1

THINK ABOUT!

Have you ever watched an athlete run a race? Have you run a race yourself? If you answered yes to either question, you may have noticed two important things. First, in order to be successful, a runner must stay on the track. Second, the runner must not have anything that slows a person down. That means no heavy clothes or big leather boots!

The writer of Hebrews 12:1 compares our Christian lives to a race. He tells us "Let us put every thing out of our lives that keeps us from doing what we should. Let us keep running in the race that God has planned for us." That's a great verse to say and pray right now!

God has called you to a race, and you can run it well by reading your Bible. That way, you'll learn what to get out of your life and what His course for you looks like.

The Bible is God's book of instructions for life. Read it every day, pray, and ask God to show you His plan for you.

PRAY!

Dear God, You have a great plan for my life, and I want to follow it every day. Please show me the things I need to get out of my life so that I can do what You want me to do. Amen.

34
MEMORIZE!

"Do for other people what you would like to have them do for you."

Luke 6:31

THINK ABOUT!

Think about things others can do for you that make you happy. Maybe it's inviting you to play with that person's friends. Or sharing a cookie from a freshly baked batch. Or maybe it's just saying something nice to you.

Jesus taught that it's good to treat others the way you want to be treated. So if you like it when people invite you to play with their friends, then invite others to play with your friends. If you like it when someone shares a cookie with you, share your snacks with others.

But there's more!

Jesus taught His followers that they should do and say nice things to others without expecting anything in return. He told them to love people and care for them. He even told them, "Love those who hate you. Do good to them" (Luke 6:35).

It's not always easy to be so kind to some people. But think about this: Jesus did the nicest thing ever when He died so that you could live in heaven forever. When He did that, He set an example for you to follow every day. You can start by saying and praying, "Do for other people what you would like to have them do for you."

PRAY!

Dear Jesus, You want me to always be nice to my family, teachers, and friends—and even to the total strangers You've put in my life. Help me think about how I would like others to treat me—and then help me treat them the very same way. Amen.

35
MEMORIZE!

O my God, take me away from those who hate me. Put me up high above those who rise up against me.

PSALM 59:1

THINK ABOUT!

In the Old Testament, God had chosen a young guy named David to serve Him as the second king of Israel. But the first king, an ungodly man named Saul, didn't like David. . .and he sure didn't want to give up his throne.

Saul knew that the people of Israel liked David—especially after David killed a giant enemy warrior named Goliath. That made Saul even more jealous, so he sent some of his soldiers to David's house. Saul didn't want them to bring David back to him. He wanted them to kill David.

David probably felt afraid of Saul (who wouldn't?), but he still trusted God to protect him. That's why he wrote in Psalm 59: "My God in His loving-kindness will meet me. God will let me look at those who come against me and know that I will win the fight" (verse 10).

You might know someone who doesn't like you and makes you feel scared, even though you've always been nice to that person. If that happens, say and pray, "O my God, take me away from those who hate me. Put me up high above those who rise up against me."

Don't forget to talk to God about your problem. Ask Him to protect you and to let you know how to solve it.

PRAY!

Dear God, when I feel worried or scared, remind me to do what David did when Saul wanted to hurt him. Remind me to bring all my problems to You because You promise to always be with me. Amen.

36
MEMORIZE!

A man cannot please God unless he has faith. Anyone who comes to God must believe that He is. That one must also know that God gives what is promised to the one who keeps on looking for Him.

HEBREWS 11:6

THINK ABOUT!

What do you think when someone makes you a promise? Like when Mom or Dad promise to take you to the park if you keep your room clean? Or when a friend promises to come over to play after school?

Promises mean a lot to us. . .and they should! When someone makes us a promise, we believe that person will follow through. So if that promise gets broken, we feel sad and hurt. We might find it hard to trust that person to keep a promise again.

People aren't perfect. Sometimes, they don't keep their promises, even when they really mean to. But you never have to worry about that with God—He *always* keeps His promises. Because He loves you, He'll never fail you. He wants you to count on Him to do every single thing the Bible says He'll do for you. The Bible is filled with thousands of promises from God. And in Hebrews 11:6, God promises to keep every one of those promises! That's why it's a good idea to say and pray, "A man cannot please God unless he has faith. Anyone who comes to God must believe that He is. That one must also know that God gives what is promised to the one who keeps on looking for Him."

Believe in God, trust God, and follow God. Then watch as He comes through for you. It really is that simple!

PRAY!

Dear God, your Word is filled with so many awesome promises for people who love You. Help me to always remember that You love me—that You want to keep all Your promises. All I need to do is keep loving and following You. Amen.

37
MEMORIZE!

*I can do all things because
Christ gives me the strength.*

Philippians 4:13

THINK ABOUT!

Following Jesus and being the kid He wants you to be isn't easy. In fact, without God's help, it's impossible!

If you've ever read God's instructions in the Bible and thought, *I can't do all that on my own*, you were right! Without Jesus and the Holy Spirit living inside you, it's impossible for you to make God happy.

That's why Jesus told His followers, "I am the Vine and you are the branches. Get your life from Me. Then I will live in you and you will give much fruit. You can do nothing without Me" (John 15:5).

Wow! What a great promise! It means that when we let Jesus live inside us, there's nothing we can't do for Him. That's what Philippians 4:13 means when it says, "I can do all things because Christ gives me the strength." That's a great promise to say and pray to God right now!

The next time you know God wants you to do something hard—like telling a friend about Jesus or being nice to someone who has been mean to you—don't tell yourself "I can't!" Instead, say, "I can do it because Jesus gives me strength!"

PRAY!

Jesus, I thank You that I get to live forever in heaven with You! And I also thank You for being with me here on earth and helping me make You happy through the way I live, talk, and think. Amen.

38
MEMORIZE!

Your thoughts are of great worth to me, O God. How many there are! If I could number them, there would be more than the sand. When I awake, I am still with You.

PSALM 139:17–18

THINK ABOUT!

The next time you're at the beach or on the banks of a river, bend down and scoop up a handful of sand. How many grains of sand would you be holding? Thousands? Tens of thousands? More? Now imagine how many handfuls of sand there are in the entire world. Is your brain ready to explode yet?

Now think about this: the Bible says that God's thoughts about you outnumber all those grains of sand! The Bible teaches that God thinks about you all the time, and He never takes His eyes off you. He loves you, and He's been thinking about you since before you were born.

That's an amazing thought, isn't it? So just say and pray, "Your thoughts are of great worth to me, O God. How many there are! If I could number them, there would be more than the sand. When I awake, I am still with You."

God always knows what you're doing or thinking. He knows when you feel happy and when you feel sad. He knows when you feel worried and when you feel peaceful. He knows all these things about you—and even better, He always *cares*.

Everything about God is incredible, especially His love for you. Because He loves you more than you can imagine, you'll never, ever have to feel like you're alone.

PRAY!

Dear Lord, there are so many people doing so many things in this world. Yet You love me more than I can understand, and You think about me all the time. You always know what I'm doing and thinking, so I'm going to think wonderful thoughts about You.

MORE GREAT DEVOTIONS FOR KIDS!

Boys and girls, ages 5 to 8, will be engaged and encouraged as they learn timeless truths about God's Word! This delightful devotional will challenge the kids in your life to run their faith race with strength and perseverance, as they're prompted to get *Ready, Set, Know Your Bible!*

Paperback / 978-1-63609-262-1